Talk to the Lioness

Poems by Barbara Daniels

Casa de Cinco
HermanasPress
Pueblo, Colorado

Casa de Cinco Hermanas Press
2315 N. Grand Ave.
Pueblo, CO 81003
www.kylelaws.com

Copyright ©Barbara Daniels, 2020
First Edition 1 3 5 7 9 10 8 6 4 2
ISBN: 978-1-950380-99-2
LCCN: 2020933258

Design, edits and layout: Kyle Laws, Jason Ryberg
Cover design: Kyle Laws
Author photo: Mark Hillringhouse
All rights reserved. No part of this publication may be reproduced or transmitted in any form or by any means, electronic or mechanical, including photocopying, recording or by info retrieval system, without prior written permission from the author.

The cover design is based on Georgia O'Keeffe's *Red Canna*, 1919 and *Lioness-Headed Goddess* 48.1560 from the Walters Art Museum collection.

TABLE OF CONTENTS

I

My God the Howler / 1

Boris the Cockatoo / 2

Sluiced / 4

Examining My Breasts / 7

The Truth about Home Remedies / 8

Circus Girl's Story / 10

Bastard Wing / 12

Tall / 13

Signs of Depression / 14

The Dead Fell Asleep / 15

Gaps / 16

The Cup / 18

Walking the Ben Franklin Bridge / 19

The Raft / 21

All Wars Memorial / 22

Tree of the Gods / 24

II

Why Am I Blind? / 27

Asking a Tea Set to Comfort Me / 28

The Light Ladder / 30

Sugaring / 32

Reading the Signs / 33

Callery Pears / 34

Looking at Churches / 35

Circumference / 36

When the Music Ends / 37

Torqued / 38

Signs You May Have an Eating Disorder / 39

Paper Snowfall / 41

Reunion / 43

More Light / 44

Back Off, Death / 46

What the Old Women Do / 47

The Snowy Owl / 49

Dancing in the Kitchen / 50

The Slotted Spoon / 52

Raffish / 54

Talk to the Lioness

I

My God the Howler

thrusts a spear through a boar's flesh,
blood, blood, heaps hair on my floor, chemo
balding, fetches reeking darkness,
my god spiteful as I am. He disdains

The Progress of the Soul. That's him
bawling overhead. Sea-washed,
he flies over whale bones, great wrecks,
Resurrection Beach Community Church.

Tell me, why am I kneeling?
My god tempts a girl to play idly
with a discarded plastic bag. He heats up
skunk cabbage, low growing, foul smelling,

so he can trap more flies. The child tugs
the bag over her head, breathes in
wet plastic. My god's a great laugher.
Snakes hang from our white mouths.

Boris the Cockatoo

I whistle while I drive my car—"Hava
Nagila," "Battle Hymn of the Republic,"
songs Jackie's cockatoo calms to, bobs
his white head as I bob mine and reaches

for me with his clawed foot. It's 18 years
since I carried tampons. I keep a photo
of me without eyebrows. Thin, I was very
thin. I lifted my soft red hat to show off

my baldness. My inner organs slumped
together where tumors large as grapefruits
crowded me. Of course Lazarus loved death.
It was dark there. Cool. He didn't have to

buy clothes or plan what to eat. There was
no weather. No boat to mend. No sisters
who would never marry. He held a round
piece of felt he made into hats: a monkey's

jingling cap, doctor's homburg, black hat
of a rich man oiled and shining. Shake
the felt! Presto, a hat covers closed
and dreaming eyes. So far I've hit and

killed a meadowlark and a pheasant, both
in refuges they might have thought safe.
I ran over a basketball while its owner stood
stricken at the side of the street. I'm a blaring

calliope strapped to the back of a gilded truck,
whistling till my mouth hurts. When I see Boris
at Jackie's house, I look straight into him—
unblinking eye, curved beak, offered claw.

Sluiced

1

I have long blonde hair like voices
of women who call from a jail
to men on the sidewalk. Like
skeins the men climb up on.

2

The day before Halloween I stand
in the bathroom, ease a blade
over my itching scalp. A thin froth
of hair sticks up from my skull
in every direction. What I keep
losing slows drains, fouls
the furniture. I look like a baby
born with a downy head or maybe
a mantis out of kilter but patient,
waiting. I have 56 staple marks
down my belly. My head is
an egg in the mirror, humbled.

3

Every hour since
the surgery
heat sluices me
I slap wet towels

*over my chest
and bald head
then fall into sleep
like a scorching ride
car windows open
to blue shimmer
highway ahead
an ocean in Iowa
glittering*

4

I struggle through chemo,
a bricked-up passage I twist and
scar myself escaping. The whole
becomes simpler than the parts:
milk warming on the stove, 6
white pills, 2 gold pills, 1 red pill,
earth tilting away from the sun.

5

I'm a cancer survivor too,
somebody tells me as I gather
books and papers and leave
a meeting, her hair abundant,
gray bangs, a smooth pageboy.
It's not just my baldness I remember,
but no eyelashes, no eyebrows,
no pubic hair. The word survivor
surprises me. I'd forgotten it.

6

What body is there but this
body clotted with age spots?

7

A woman washes my hair
in a black basin, black plastic
cape protecting me. She talks
about her hair loss, chemo,
radiation, touching me
tenderly. On the floor my cut
hair forms a soft pale fan.

Examining My Breasts

Some women wait till their tumors bulge
like oranges. They juggle their breasts
into their dresses, never look, never touch,
wait months till they see a doctor
in Oklahoma City, go home in the pickup the day
of the surgery, make Thanksgiving dinner
with draining tubes tucked in their clothes.

I knew a woman who threw away
garter belts and pushup bras so her children
wouldn't have to after she died. She called
a doctor the day she found the lump,
walked out on the grass to talk
with her surgeon, did what he told her,
and died though she was careful.

When I lift my arms, veins in my armpits
twine in a web. I slide my fingers
over my breasts. I fear dead ends,
no way out. I make myself follow
the shuddering paths, brush
my way in where a spider waits,
one foot testing a sticky strand.

The Truth about Home Remedies

If you have a heart like a tinderbox,
a mind like an old cash register, open
a guide to ships. Mark your text

so you know when to breathe. Do you
feel like a bolus the attic spit up
and rolled down the folding stairs?

It might be wise to avoid fierce sunlight
and clouds helpless as beached whales.
What's in the cupboard? Space

between plate and plate. A cup,
a mouse. Or the idea of mouse, full of
cunning and disease—there

by the beans, oatmeal, tea. Is
someone out in the weeds coughing,
banging the gate? There is a remedy.

That nodule on your elbow is nothing.
Smear it with lemon oil. Touch your body
as if all you're doing is signing your name.

Raise your face for kisses like insects.
Light falls from your window
to the ground. Tulips stir like caged

birds. Look at the leaves like new
paper money. Rattle the rings and
bracelets you stole from the dead.

Here where a wine stain never came out
of the carpet, repeat the names of ships—
Argo, Pilgrim, the pinnace Disdain.

Circus Girl's Story

I ran away from the circus. I'd braved
the flimsy basketwork swing and
swaying wire. A clown taught me

to put on flopping shoes, a bulbous nose.
He showed me his winterberry mouth,
his plum eyes. Hoopers, jugglers, I

was their changeling. I read to them
or pretended to, ran my hand down a page
but told my own story—girl with

a needle who comes while you sleep,
girl who turns herself into a mower,
rolls forward, glistens, clacks her enemy

under her turning sickle-bar and spits
him out minus an eyebrow or earlobe.
I told death stories—a flaming stake,

the vast iced north. An acrobat helped
me walk on my hands. The trick rider
grabbed me, stood me up on a bay

horse's back, and slapped its rump.
When I fell, I was part of the act,
the magnificent death drag. Did I

kiss someone? Did he touch me?
The top of the tent hid the trembling
sky. I went to talk to the lioness.

The calliope switched to a minor key.
The lioness huffed and snuffled, her
tongue a bold rubber muscle. She told

me to run for it. I left my carbon-fiber
jumping stilts, spinning plates, shining
knives. But I still breathe fire.

Bastard Wing

A fire hydrant looks like the street's thick
thumb, next to it the feral woman,
the one who never washes. She tells me

birds have alulae, bastard wings. I've
heard of bastard sandalwood, fat
bastard typeface, bastard wine. Alulae?

She says they're quills birds lift to keep from
stalling. Most days she stands on the corner,
strikes up conversations, tries to sell

her battered books. I see she's thinner,
the books more worn. Even the shop fronts
seem narrowed. She says she gives up

till all that's left sometimes is one note
played on a cello, too high, too thin. To get
that note, she says to touch a fingerboard

precisely, lightly, first at the halfway point,
then higher, higher till the harmonic
whistles above this city, this humbled street.

Tall

A woman grows taller and taller till
she looms above her friends, brushes
her head on doorframes, grows
out of her sensible clothes. She
transmits unease like an altered
photograph—too-red barn, arc-lit
church, water so blurred and
brightened it gleams like tinfoil.
Doctors say it's nothing: late-life
growth spurt, slow-motion
shipwreck, and now her head
rises out of the moonroof
as she drives her car. Her lips
murmur, her empurpled heart. She
pivots her head, identifies beech trees,
sees the young in their tiny clothes.
Leaves tumble like laundry. She wants
objects to stop leaping forward, shiny
with meaning like dropped forks.
She sees how it ends, her head
twinned to the scarred moon,
one hand touching down in Iowa,
one in New Jersey, and all around
the unearthly music of the spheres.

Signs of Depression

Those were the months when sadness made her thin.
What is the word for sorrow with no cause?
She took in her clothes and took them in again.

She gave herself to nights with teeth of tin
that slit her heart and chewed on all her flaws.
Those were the months when sadness made her thin.

She dressed herself in skirts of onion skin
and turned in the mirror, hearing no applause.
She took in her clothes, then took them in again.

Hers was a life betrayed by discipline,
by pills in a box and echoing guffaws. Those
were the months when sadness made her thin.

She felt like a dusty, empty mannequin
with plastic beads for eyes, hands made of straw.
She took in her clothes and took them in again.

She fixed up her face and painted on a grin
married to melancholy and its laws. Those
were the months when sadness kept her thin.
She took in her clothes, then took them in again.

The Dead Fell Asleep

for David

Killings occurred that were not themselves
political. The ocean slid onto sand
and stopped there. People wrote poems
the wind blew away. The dead
left invisible lines on the pavement.

I think you remember sun in your hair,
waves frothing and sliding.
You studied the movement of water,
the secret hegemony of the trees.
I watched the light on that month's

massing of skin cells, that year's bones
in your face. The dead fell asleep
face up in their coffins. Specialists
interviewed witnesses. Loons spread
the chill with their distant cries.

Politicians touched their soft mouths,
blinking mechanically. I saw you
turn from the flashing lights
to look toward a spiral galaxy
wheeling four times in a million years.

Gaps

> *aposiopesis* A sudden break in the middle
> of a sentence, the speaker unwilling
> or unable to continue

There's a name for it, a speaker
   stopped; she can't or won't
      continue. But what's the word

for loving a place you had to leave?
   And the word that means needing
      a story, however false, that lust

for narrative? And what about this—
   haven't you done this?—
      driven up to the wrong house

months after a breakup, but you're
   tired, it's late, and part of your mind
      forgets where you live, the brave

apartment, cat, row of narrow windows.
   Here's a term: deadheading, a woman
      snapping browned flowers

to force new growth or merely tidy, the habit
   of order out in the garden. But what
      of the 25,000 who die each day

of starvation? Gaps appear, a newswoman's
    breathing. She reads us her story: An African
    named her daughter Forget.

The Cup

I tried to make friends with a cup.
First with my hand
in a dark glove. Then my skin
touched its rough surface.
I was trying to cross
a river out of this world.

The cup calmly refused me,
stronger than grief. I was
a woman in wartime, head
shaved for collaboration,
hair on the floor in soft piles
stirred by booted feet.

My cup turned its hard shoulder,
facing away. It carried water
as it always did but would not
comfort my dry lips, would
not give solace
to my bleeding hands.

Walking the Ben Franklin Bridge

Rows of lights glow in their metal
cages. My body gently collapses,
bones thinning, ulcers forming
on my gums. I hear my heart

as I climb the cold metal stairs.
The stone in Ben Franklin made
travel an agony. Attendants lifted
him onto a litter, stowaway stone

alert in his bladder. Instead of
Paris—opium, home, a lavish funeral.
In Christ Church graveyard, the stone
lies in dirt, held in the curve of his pelvis.

I'd like to send resonant low notes
out over water and back to tilting
tombstones. Barbed wires guard
New Jersey Transit's shining rails,

the snow so wet it falls in clumps,
melting already on my face and arms.
I'd like to have nothing to wake me
at 3 AM. I could turn over now,

suspended within the harp of the bridge,
suffused with the sweetness of sleep,
snowflakes mere afterthoughts,
nothing, something, then nothing again.

The Raft

Everyone's dead or dying
in Gericault's painting. He locked
himself up with corpses. Emptied
a room, backed benches to walls.
An eye stared into nacreous light.

How do peasants die, Tolstoy asked
as he, a nobleman, embarked
on his dying. Deserted crossroads,
invisible coach in the distance, man
turned to still life, action arrested.

Night pressed in, raft half seen,
half imagined, trees the wind
abandoned, clouds layered pale
over dark. Waves deepened
and lifted, tipping the laden raft.

All Wars Memorial
Logan Square, Philadelphia

I watch a man sweep steps with last night's gray
blanket, clearing snow from the soldiers' monument—
a torch, four eagles, a figure of Justice lifting

wreaths that symbolize honor. Black soldiers
in uniform turn toward her, forming *a lasting
record of their unselfish devotion to duty.*

The man straightens a wreath from Viet Nam vets,
its pistils and sepals curling. Tonight will be cold.
When will he sleep? Trees clot white, snow

relentless. I touch my hand as if it's a stranger's.
All these bits of me, atom and long-shot cold
in the half-light. My mother gave food away

at our back door to men too humbled to come
to the front. She'd been through dust storms and
the terrible wastes of the Depression. *God bless*

you, someone said to her. I watched him eat
his sandwich, jaw like a snake's swallowing some
small animal. Smoke from a flaming tanker

blocks from here spreads down this city street. What poisons move on the wind into our eyes and mouths? Emergency vehicles cannonball past. Doors jut open.

I walk closer to see. The man brushes the steps over and over, his blanket clearing an O for the wreath. Blown snow acts out a pantomime: *run, pivot, fall.*

Tree of the Gods

Or so it's called—ailanthus—forgetting
that gods are prone to accidents,
the world awash with sticky liquid,
fog drop-curtained over the city
as if a sky god spilled beer.

The ailanthus grows six feet a year,
stretches up toward the dirtied dome
of the sky. In the tree of the gods
chickadees sing, but it's an invader,
crowding roadsides and empty lots.

An urban tree harbors inclusions
(nails, wires, clothes hooks)
so sawmills don't want it. Some
people call it the tree of hell,
hating its stinking blossoms.

They can't kill it, can't stop
its suckers from breaking pavement,
taking down walls. But after wars,
the ailanthus rises in rubble.
When its leaves open, it's spring.

II

Why Am I Blind?

The last words of my friend's mother
were *Oh shit.* My mother's were
You are forgiven when Sandra

bumped her, changing her Depends,
doing the ritual turning. *Why
am I blind?* Mom had asked.

Because you're dying, I'd said.
*Your senses are failing. But
I'm told you'll hear us till the end.*

*How long will it take? You mean
till you die?* The doctors thought
one more day. When I asked Sandra

to sing for Mom, it was "Amazing
Grace," a great rich river of sound
as if we were standing in church.

Mom slept then. Or seemed
to be sleeping. I touched her arm.
Sandra left the room sobbing.

Asking a Tea Set to Comfort Me

I move dishes around the kitchen,
soiled, clean, this is grief, fill
a shelf with shining glassware, pour

out curdled milk. Playing house
required small dishes, sticks
to stir mudcakes, Mom's hats

and soft shawl for dress-up. Real
house proved to be similar: plates
and bowls, rickety chairs, canned

peas, pale toast, a glass of gin too small
and weak to hearten me. The furnace
broke. Cold seeps in. Would the dead

sneer if they knew I still have
my little tin tea set? A needle rides
an old record, a dead woman

sings Strauss's last songs. I've played
out the rope of me, hand over hand.
My life is a frozen fish stick,

a chicken nugget fuzzed with ice.
There's a mirror in the freezer. I look
in to see what's inside me—red

throat, iced-up heart. My ancestors
lived through the plague—farm
women wearing velvet gowns

stripped from corpses. I fear
the plague, and I dress for it—
this red velvet, this silver chain.

The Light Ladder

My friends and I have failing hearts
and some bad prognoses. Anxieties
buzz us like fruit flies. Our faces
look like hard cheese. I read that

three genes determine the sex
of a fruit fly—deadpan, sex-lethal,
sisterless. I'm my own old person
now. It's my schedule of doctors

I scan, studying each deadpan,
sex-lethal, sisterless illness.
Sometimes I can't climb into
the big black balloon of sleep

so I'm still awake when sunrise
lights jittery grass as if for an opera.
The side of my face that caught
the sun as I drove toward the west

is crumpling. My friends forget things.
But they still dance to a jazz quartet,
songs I can't quite identify. I'm
the one clapping at the wrong times,

smiling like an outdated Kennedy.
I prefer days like blank pages
that fill out the backs of books.
I wish I could phone myself,

full of love and sound advice
or a scant teaspoon of empathy,
then drive to a refuge where
thousands of cranes bugle,

leap, rise up together. Light
ladders down through blinds
to my floor. A wind chime clinks,
the one a friend made out of knives.

Sugaring

On River Road, I find a $10.94
Facts Plus pregnancy test box,
soaked instructions beside it. It's icy,

treacherous. Men are sugaring by the river,
checking tree spouts and sap buckets,
tending a fire, drinking midmorning beers.

Propped in ice on the roadway,
a broken bowl holds a blue candle.
I think a girl must have left it to burn.

Perhaps her breasts are sore or numb now.
She may feel unexpectedly tired. The best
weather for sugaring is warm days

like today, freezing nights. Stones gleam
in meltwater cascading out of a culvert.
There's no sign of the urine collection cup,

urine dropper, test disk, foil pouch.
The river is higher than I've ever seen it.
I think the girl may feel dizzy or faint.

She may start to cry for no reason. It's sugaring
season, too late to compact the trail snow, to run
the heavy dragger with spring-loaded blades.

Reading the Signs

You tell me the mark
on a dragonfly's wing
is a stigma, tattoo mark,
the plural stigmata,
bloody holes in the body
of Christ. Ice covers
the road at Skunk Hollow.
I want you to climb
the pock-marked hills
where snow is about to
let go. You say Nkondi
figures—I've seen them—
are African objects
studded with nails,
medicine hidden
in mirrored bellies,
each new spike a sign
of an oath. We've had
our losses, but you claim
spring is entelechy—
wholeness. We've been
thumbscrewed
by cold, but spring,
I swear it, comes
in budbreak, amber
to willows, red
to the tips of the elms.

Callery Pears

Wind flails blooms, knocking petals
into grass. Judas said, *Lord, why are you*

laughing at us? Winter birds, fat at my feeder,
disappear night by night, gone north.

Mom said, *No one has to look at me
after I die*, and I didn't. At the end

I counted the seconds between breaths,
said goodbye instead of good night.

Judas saw a luminous cloud.
What good is it? he said.

So many Callery pears blossom in fields
and near houses. Their white froth

sweeps through the suburbs. We're told
not to plant them, their branches wrong

for snow and storms. The great trees,
a red oak, a black oak, gather themselves

to sail through another summer, lift
new leaves like glowing bits of glass.

Judas said, *Does the human spirit die?*

Looking at Churches

I wake. Put on this body,
the ache of it, soft palms,
rough skin of my elbows.
I eat more bread dripped

with honey, change the rags
beside the leaking dishwasher,
move as if caught by glue, sticky
residue of days in the car.

I've been looking at churches,
spires on raw prefab rectangles,
brick churches all down
the Eastern Shore, effigies,

fonts, crosses, flames.
Abundant Life Restoration
Center, Joshua Chapel,
Harmony Missionary Baptist,

Zion United, New Hope.
I'm afraid of the hollowing
Mom's death made in me.
I want a new season in throats

of birds, fields of fluorescent
green, reflections that leap from
the surface of water, wavering
shadows, columns of light.

Circumference

I wish I were one of the great walkers,
Saint Paul wearing dusty sandals, Wordsworth
in a yellow tie. Cezanne walked eight
or nine miles a day, lugging
equipment, climbing low hills.

Charles Wright says everything tends
toward circumference. I take that to mean
his walking in circles, the Blue Ridge,
the dark yard. The scale shifts at night,
rivers of constellations revolving,

the lame getting up to walk, meres
and rivers black as obsidian. It's possible
Paul walked ten thousand miles.
I'll never catch up now. A swallow
snags a bit of white fluff, then lets it go.

It inhabits the air's narrow sphere
along with gasses and particulates. I draw
a horizon line in charcoal, make a moon
out of paper mâché. I see how the world is—
stunned by the heat of an August day.

When the Music Ends

Years after your death a magazine
emailed: *We want you back, Viola.*
Today, a little morning rain. You told me

before you met Dad you walked sedately
past the bank where he worked, turned
the corner, took off your shoes, and ran.

Why he married you: that blazing hair.
When I looked like an egg, no eyebrows,
no lashes, some people laughed at me.

Just last night a waitress said, *Sorry, sir,*
mistaking my tousled hair and androgynous
shirt. My streaming service wrote me:

*When your music ends, we will continue
to play music you should like.* As you
were dying, your friend said, *You*

have the best hair in the building.
Still red in your ninety-ninth year.
When I die, my atoms could leap into

fingers and feet. I might be somebody's
shining hair. It's raining, but softly.
Mahler's third symphony plays.

Torqued

I'm entirely faithless, nothing left
of sweaty childhood Sundays
but the smell of snuffed candles

and rotting lilies, clatter of kneelers.
Sometimes I think a soul looks
sideways out of a face, a gleam

of consciousness shot my way.
Some souls thrive in a monk's cell,
a cave like the one that housed

St. Francis after he quit running
naked, having stripped off his cloak,
tunic, shoes. Surprise me, Lord.

I might still believe in the cold
sunrise that lights up the highway's
road kills. My story isn't important,

just the usual cancers and
heart-frying deaths. My spirit's
been torqued by pincers, spanners,

breaker bars. Can someone
please pick up a crescent wrench
and twist till it lets in some light?

Signs You May Have an Eating Disorder

White clay you chew through
before you get back to your car.
Dirt. A pair of dice that clatter

across a long table. Paper.
Paint chips. Drywall. Hair.
Burnt matches. Hemlock

you touch to your lips,
thinking fennel, thinking
anise. You yank mushrooms

out of the rot and stuff them
into your mouth. A spider spins
protein into cogs and wands.

You hear gypsy moth larvae
chewing. Look, evening
like a plateful of cake.

Chocolate light, moist air.
Lightning flickers.
A possum skitters. Now

you can open your jewelry box
and take out a tipped disk
of lumpy pearls formed

in gold-lipped oysters. And
your favorites, cultured pearls
smooth and sour as lemon drops.

Paper Snowfall

A ceiling fan whispers, flips
pages of scattered books. I look at
my scarred body naked, dress it
in new black pants, old black shoes,

my inwardness like a cat's,
likewise my vanity. I feel the prick
of appetite, hear an inner piano
pound out Thelonious Monk.

It's just early old age, I tell myself.
When I was young, I had cowboy
boots, plastic chaps, a red feathered
hat. I listened to the tale of the toad.

I folded and cut with snubbed
scissors—girls holding hands
flung out in a chain—paper
snowfall on my arms and sifting

down to the dirty floor. Iron bands
bound my heart. I was a wall,
a ticking clock, a chalk-white child
in a poodle skirt. Tell me, toad,

what time is it? I used to stand
at the edge of a cliff, waving. I'm
on the last ship now, sounding
the tuning fork of the stars.

Reunion

Nobody told me my cousin Melody died.
Leah is eight. She says her cat's dying.
She's old for a cat, Leah tells me.

All but two of her chickens and both
her rabbits were killed by a dog
that tore through chicken wire.

One of my third cousins says she has five
children and she herself was a fifth child.
How is it you have no children, she asks me.

How terrible. What terrible thing
went wrong. What animals do you have
at home, Leah asks. Her last chicken's neck

got twisted around. Uncle Nick died.
And Mickie. Aunt Grace. I knew that.
Nobody told me Melody died.

Now that Mom's dead, nobody calls
with the family news. Leah, I have no
animals. No chickens, cats, rabbits, dogs.

More Light

I used to ask friends if they
were happy. We lifted mouths
of bottles to our mouths, spoke

about men and their secret
gentleness. Now we talk about
knees and hearts. A bird stays

at my feeder, leans on the iced
cylinder of seeds. It's clear—
this cold is too strong for it.

As a bird dies, it looks for
a place to squeeze itself into,
last chance to hide. The day rivers

through me. I boil eggs, peel
them, chop them for sandwiches,
listen to Bach in the steady current,

days longer but colder, dirt hard,
and under the ice, dark water
moving. At a bar, drinking,

my friends and I planned our last
words—*More light* or *Either
that wallpaper goes or I do.*

I chose *I lower my head and
plunge into death*. Maybe I'll
be forgiving every transgression

or asking for beer. Vultures
knock snow from branches,
doing what they should do—

eating the dead. As they tear
at a roadkill, sunlight
bleaches the rising ground.

Back Off, Death

Give back the IV drip. Life
wants to put on her fur hip belt,
finger cymbals, glitter lipstick.

Stop laughing at grief days,
people lined up like penitents,
crying like refugees. Life is

researching which panties
look best with a twelve-inch skirt.
When you tip the floor up,

she can slide on it. Didn't you
used to have better sacraments,
the dying girded for final

journeys, slathered with
sweet-smelling oil? Stop watching
the hanging woman, hair blown

over her bloated face. Teach me
to dance like a crane, awkward,
ecstatic, arms lifted like wings.

What the Old Women Do

Stains on our skirts, frayed gray hair,
we take balls of red thread
into the neighborhood to tie up
tulips and mad forsythia. We haven't

completely lost our cars, edging our way
through hilly lots, swatting at bees.
Sometimes we wake up screaming.
Were we running like thieves

all these years, just not knowing
we were dreaming? We see the way earth
and death look alike—tongues touch
top teeth, mouths slacken.

Weeds volunteer, green from the waking
ground. We hear shifting sounds
dead people make. Pine, old whisperer,
sweet in your constancy, we beckon you

out of the darkness. We see in the stars
a sky-spanning hand, gems on its fingers
and wrist, women with talons
instead of feet, faces like our faces,

star born. We eat animals and they
eat us, worms cleaning skeletons.
Vultures pull apart bodies laid out
on a midden, ten thousand clam shells

and human bones. Look over the water
to white wings lifting and falling. Do you
see avocets? Or women street dancing,
striking our feet on concrete?

The Snowy Owl

I walk down a long roofless corridor, trees
close on either side of me, stars in my hair,
moon poked by twigs and branches.

In a flat clump of cordgrass
Athena's white owl turns its head
nearly around. What that means—

hard flight from the distant north,
voles snapped in its beak. This is
the world's work, labored flight, bloody

dying. What gods can do—bind
with vines, turn us to stone so cold and
smooth people run fingers over our thighs.

What does the moon's silver signify?
What kind of value? My friend wants
his ashes strewn on the pitcher's mound

at the town park and secretly spooned
on his mother's grave. My ashes?
Just shake the bag out. Atoms will scatter

like flying sparks. Night enlarges.
Wind brushes clouds aside. The owl
rises, a noiseless sweep of pale wings.

Dancing in the Kitchen

Another woman slept here. Lovely,
our friend says though he won't
say her name. Perhaps she cooked.
Perhaps they drank and danced.

I found the radio set to a Russian station.
When my father was forgetting
everything, he wanted sex every day.
He forgot the day before and the day

before that. Doctor Cohen told Mom
he'd heard this from younger couples.
Dad was 84. The doctor said
Mom could say no. Maybe she did.

I have a husband who loves me.
That helps me bless what love there is,
what desiring, hot oil in a pan,
fragrance of garlic filling the kitchen,

pork that spatters and burns my fingers.
Our friend watched the house
while my husband and I drove toward
turning leaves and surf bursting on stones.

It's as if the house is a secret
snow leopard that only gets wilder
if no one is watching. They're all dead
now: my mother, her ten brothers

and sisters, my father, his brother,
that brother's wife. Yet there is still
desiring, dance music, pork with fig sauce,
and a strange toothbrush left by the sink.

The Slotted Spoon

The street lights still on, not yet
dawn, I walk in fog light, draggling
through defeated leaves. I found the watch
I lost, right where it belonged, tucked
in with my bracelets and rings.

Morning starts to smell like church—
damp earth, starched shirts. The gingkoes
lost all their leaves last night. Somebody
pulled a thread, and the whole yellow
apparatus flung itself down. We have

enough seasons. Sometimes they shine
and sometimes they're more about
absence—lost tree, unmarked grave.
The gods now are just like the heroes,
suet-faced, blurred, wayward weaklings.

The sun fails. Birdsong fails. The parts
have been simplified so anyone
can play them. A man stops in the fog
to name the animals—squirrels,
groundhogs. Only the fog asks

the right question: What's worth
remembering? Above the chords of an old
hymn, my mother sings, dipping out
carrots with her slotted spoon.
Come in, she sings. All is prepared.

Raffish

In the last hushed hour
before waking, silk garments
slip from my body, lavender,

green, teal, black, plum
until I am no one, perfectly
indolent. Let's stick with

the sacred acts: first kiss
at daybreak, the newspaper,
coffee. I've worked out

what raffish means, dirtied dish,
your unshaven almost piratical face.
In the bedroom under the eaves,

crumpled paper, socks, lint,
books—disreputable but
attractive. Today has the ease

of summer, casting off clothes,
bare legs and arms, our crooked
feet. One leaf on the ivy

curls upward, waiting to open.
Let's agree to agree. August
is for this—placating

the body, letting the hours
slow and subside. Tell me
what you always tell me,

those endearments, the blue
walls shadowed to gray,
the yellow ones struck by light.

Barbara Daniels's Rose Fever was published by WordTech Press and her chapbooks *Moon Kitchen, Black Sails* and *Quinn & Marie* by Casa de Cinco Hermanas Press. Her chapbook *The Woman Who Tries to Believe* won the Quentin R. Howard Prize from Wind Publications. She received three Individual Artist Fellowships from the New Jersey State Council on the Arts and earned an MFA in poetry at Vermont College. Her poems have appeared in *Prairie Schooner, Mid-American Review, WomenArts Quarterly Journal, The Literary Review,* and many other journals. Barbara has taught at the middle school, high school, and college level. She and her husband David I. Daniels wrote two textbooks, English Grammar and Persuasive Writing, published by HarperCollins.

Acknowledgments:

Grateful acknowledgment is made to the following publications where these poems or earlier versions of them first appeared:

Apricity, "The Slotted Spoon"; *Barnstorm Literary Journal*, "Signs You May Have an Eating Disorder"; *Briar Cliff Review*, "Raffish"; *The Cape Rock*, "Dancing in the Kitchen"; *Casa de Cinco Hermanas*, "Gaps," "The Snowy Owl"; *Chiron Review*, "Callery Pears"; *Clare*, "Signs of Depression"; *Cleaver*, "Tall"; *The Cortland Review*, "Sugaring"; *Earth's Daughters*, "Reading the Signs"; *Edison Literary Review*, "Looking at Churches"; *Freshwater*, "Tree of the Gods," "Why Am I Blind?"; *Journal of New Jersey Poets*, "Paper Snowfall"; *Kentucky Review*, "What the Old Women Do"; *Misfit Magazine*, "Back Off, Death"; *MO: Writings From the River*, "The Cup"; *Moria*, "Torqued"; *Philadelphia Poets*, "Walking the Ben Franklin Bridge"; *Philadelphia Stories*, "Boris the Cockatoo," "When the Music Ends"; *Prairie Schooner*, "My God the Howler"; *Sonic Boom*, "The Dead Fell Asleep"; *Summerset Review*, "Circus Girl's Story"; *Tattoo Highway*, "Reunion"; *Two Hawks Quarterly*, "The Raft"; *Wait a Minute, I Have to Take Off My Bra*, "Examining My Breasts"

Thank you to The Virginia Center for the Creative Arts and The Vermont Studio Center for time and space to work on these poems. Thanks to Sundress Press for including "Sugaring" in Best of the Net 2013, to Casa de Cinco Hermanas Press for publishing "Sugaring" in *Quinn and Marie*, and to Taylor Savath and Ona Gritz for including "Gaps" and "Confounded" in the anthology *Welcome to the Resistance!*

And special thanks to the friends who helped me with these poems and (as always) to my husband, David I. Daniels.